I LOVE ME

A Book of Healing

Yuki

Yuki's Art & Language

Gold Coast, Australia

Copyright © 2020 by Yuki's Art & Language

All rights reserved. No part of this publication may be reproduced, distributed or transmitted in any form or by any means, without prior written permission.

Yuki's Art & Language
PO Box 3301, Australia Fair
QLD, Australia
www.yukisartandlanguage.com

I LOVE ME / Yuki's Art & Language. -- 1st ed.
ISBN 978-0-6488108-1-0

Dedication to my daughter and me

Contents

DRAGON'S MOON AND ME 2
CENTRED SELF VS. SELFISH 4
REACH INSIDE 8
BE HONEST WITH YOUR FEELINGS 10
LOOKING INSIDE MY EMOTIONS, BECAUSE I CARE 12
YOUR PEARL 14
NEVER SUCH THING AS TOO 'SENSITIVE' 16
MOMENTS OF MY LIFE 18
A LIFE FORMED FROM TEARS 20
MY SACRED PLACE 22
MY HAPPY PLACE 24
I AM WHERE I AM 26
AUTHENTICITY - BE YOURSELF 28
I WISH YOU HAPPINESS 30
I LOVE ME, SO 32

Dragon's Moon and Me

There is a place where your dreams can manifest.

It is a place beyond what's been told.

It is a journey to find this place.

It takes practice to be in this place.

Open your eyes.

Open your heart.

For what you are looking for, this place is right here, inside you.

CENTRED SELF vs. SELFISH

All things have a fine line.

'The other side of the coin' refers to the duality of things. Every trait has positive and negative aspects. Although 'positive' and 'negative' are subjective, there is always a higher frequency and lower frequency expression of a trait. The shadow and the light of the same entity are 'both sides of the coin'.

Being 'selfish' is not the same side as being a centred self. Being 'selfish' and being self-centred are two sides of the same coin, and therefore the opposite of each other. Although they are both focusing on the self, the lower vibration expression of this is 'selfish'. To be 'selfish' is to focus only on one's own needs through a narrow perspective and at the expense of others. Self-centredness is the higher vibration expression of this. Being self-centred is to focus on understanding yourself, identifying your needs and meeting them.

So, know that centring the self is being the opposite of a selfish user, controller or manipulator.

It is the only way to find your heart.

It is the individual's responsibility to oneself to find one's centre. To ask: what does my heart say? What do I want?

REACH INSIDE

To find your heart, you need to reach inside.

Under the moonlight, our wishes reside. They are fuzzy, curious and joyful.

Outside influences may have suppressed them.

So look inside to find your feelings.

What do I want for me?

This question itself is the hand reaching in.

From within, it activates your life force.

BE HONEST WITH YOUR FEELINGS

People may not understand how you feel. But at least you can know how you feel.

It all starts with being honest with your feelings.

How does your body react to it? Whatever it is, take notice.

Do you feel relaxed? Excited? Happy? Or not?

It's not about judging yourself or forcing yourself to feel a certain way.

It's about being honest with yourself, being honest with how you feel.

Recognizing that feeling is a big start.

Just acknowledging the feeling and being there for you, within you, is the whole point of living as you.

Be Honest with your *Feelings*

LOOKING INSIDE MY EMOTIONS, BECAUSE I CARE...

Looking inside our emotions can be hard.

Only when we care, can we muster the courage to look inside ourselves.

It takes commitment to care for the self.

To care for the self, go beyond the fear of the unknown and feel the pool of 'life'.

Those different emotions you experience before, after and at present are all the products of your life.

Emotion has created a pool of life experience, and you're in it. That is what we came here to experience: life and emotion.

YOUR PEARL

When you dive into the ocean of emotion, you will find your original innocence you had before you were hurt.

It lives untouched and pure, deep inside still.

Your pearl is waiting for you to find it.

It has been there the whole time, maturing its beauty.

Your pearl is waiting for you to grow and have the courage to find it.

This pearl is there for you to find it.

Dive into the ocean of emotion and find your pearl

NEVER SUCH THING AS TOO 'SENSITIVE'

In the journey to accessing our own emotions, all our senses awaken along the way.

It may take some time to get used to this new sense of 'feeling so much'.

But know that there is never such thing as too sensitive. Being sensitive means you are aware of something. There is just more you are aware of, and from there, you can choose what you want to do with it.

Sometimes our memories and traumas create 'dramatic' surges in our emotions. People may see this as being dramatic or too sensitive, but it is merely acting by our own emotion.

So remember and know that there is never such thing as too sensitive. Your reaction to something is 100% valid and reasonable for your context. Be there for you.

When we accept this, we can have more choice of what we want to do with our sensitivity.

So, with all that you are aware of, you have more choice of what you want to do.

Never such thing as too "sensitive" there's just more you can be aware of. Your choice what to do with it 🩷

MOMENTS OF MY LIFE

Looking at moments of your life should amaze you.

You will find yourself everywhere within your world.

You are always there in your memories.

You were always with you.

Every moment, it was you.

It was all about you.

All the experiences show you who you are.

This life is all about living with you.

Giving you a chance to get to know you, more consciously.

So you can embrace more of who you are.

A LIFE FORMED FROM TEARS

Sometimes in life, unfortunate things happen.

So, let your tears wash and nurture you as much as you need.

A life formed from tears is pure, gentle and loving.

You can see it when you come out of your tears.

A field of new shoots awaits you.

You have watered them.

They are your creation.

Your tears have been watering the seeds of your wishes.

A Life formed from tears...
You can see it when you come out of your tears

MY SACRED PLACE

Always find your 'sacred place'. It's a place where you can close your eyes and breathe in peace, safe from the outside world.

Feel the existence of yourself and your surroundings. Relax and enjoy the moment. This sacred place is within you.

It is a place before the worries and the criticisms that consumed you.

It is a place of your true happiness and joy. It is the initial excitement.

In nature, in your room, in your mind, find your sacred place.

Dream with your original feelings.

Embrace that feeling. If it feels good, then you are in your sacred place.

MY HAPPY PLACE

In my happy place, I live with my beautiful animals.

Even during the 'heck of a journey', I am connecting with my happy place.

So I know, 'what I like' and 'what I want to protect'.

My happy place is where I get my energy to keep going.

Where is your happy place?

It is worth creating, protecting and living with every day.

I AM WHERE I AM

When we centre the self and go with the flow, we have a better idea of where we are.

We want to get to the state of mind, 'I know where I am'.

Not in a 'selfish' way. This state is the other side of the coin to that. It is about being modest with you and centring yourself.

It is an honest, feeling-based, conscious awareness; blatantly honest "this is where I am".

Whenever you are in this state of mind, you have more clarity to give you what you need.

You align with yourself and align with the Universal flow.

AUTHENTICITY - BE YOURSELF

The bottom line is, there is nothing to lose other than the self.

We are all alone and unique individuals, but that is because 'we are one'. Paradoxically in physical life, we are all experiencing an illusion of separation.

Feeling alone is the reflection of authenticity as 'One' and also the illusion of separation.

In our physical life journey, we have individual experiences again and again. Whatever way the journey goes, we are seekers of our authenticity. We want to be who we truly are.

So be yourself, the authentic you.

There is nothing to lose other than the self.

Authenticity   Be with yourself

There is nothing to lose
other
than
the
self

I WISH YOU HAPPINESS!!

I wish you happiness!!

The Universe can support your happiness if you wish. So, ask for it and walk your journey with the signs, messages and feelings on your side.

Be kind to yourself and make wishes for your happiness.

Feel the happiness of living as you, more and more.

Ultimately, we want to feel the happiness of being 'who we are'. But at the very least, in that process, continue to love and care for yourself every day.

I wish you happiness

That includes
♡ authentic ♡
You being you!
You loving being you
You creating your joyful path
You enjoy walking it
Smelling flowers & fresh air

Enjoy your journey

I LOVE ME, SO...

It takes a commitment to love yourself.

But if you can commit, you've got someone so reliable on your side.

That is you.

When you are there for you, magic happens.

You emanate beautiful energy.

You can happily regenerate yourself.

You are then an autonomous individual, a mastered self, being ready for interdependence.

Connecting to the self and happily connecting with others.

I love me, so

I will always listen to my feelings
I will always take care of me
I will never give up on me
I will always pick me up no matter what
I will always look after me

www.yukisartandlanguage.com
@yukisartlanguage